**■SCHOLASTIC**

Best Practices in Action

# Fluency Practice Mini-Books

## GRADE 3

By KATHLEEN M. HOLLENBECK

NEW YORK • TORONTO • LONDON • AUCKLAND • SYDNEY
MEXICO CITY • NEW DELHI • HONG KONG • BUENOS AIRES

**Teaching** *Resources*

*To the patient*

*and dedicated teachers*

*who guide*

*and encourage students.*

Cover design by Maria Lilja
Interior design by Kathy Massaro
Interior art by Margeaux Lucas, Bari Weissman, Nadine Bernard Wescott, and Jenny Williams

ISBN: 0-439-55418-7
Copyright © 2005 by Kathleen M. Hollenbeck.
Published by Scholastic Inc.
All rights reserved.
Printed in the U.S.A.

2 3 4 5 6 7 8 9 10    40    13 12 11 10 09 08 07 06 05

# Contents

# INTRODUCTION

As educators, we believe there is power inherent in the written word. It is the power of knowledge and interaction—the ability to convey what we mean and to be heard, the gift that brings others' thoughts into our realm of understanding. It is our hope that the children in our care will learn to look to the written word for the same reasons we do—to answer questions, clarify learning, and exchange ideas.

A relationship between readers and the text can come only from training and experience. To help unlock the meaning of language, we teach readers to apply sense to symbols. They learn to associate sounds with letters and then to combine letters to make words. Ultimately, they connect these words to make sense of what they are reading. They can answer questions such as "What is this story about?" and "What is the author telling me?"

For some, this progression happens naturally. One day children are decoding single words and the next they are reading sentences, paragraphs, and chapters with ease. For others, each step comes with great effort, and success is not always at hand. They seek what the proficient readers have—and what all readers deserve: fluency.

Fluency, the ability to read with speed, accuracy, and expression, is essential to comprehension, which is the primary goal of reading. Fluency comes with practice, and all readers must strive to achieve it. Readers who are already fluent, readers who are well on their way to being so, and those who are struggling to get there all must employ practice and patience to become confident, capable readers. Their skills may be different, but their goal is the same: They want to understand.

This teaching resource, *Fluency Practice Mini-Books: Grade 3*, offers countless opportunities to build and strengthen your students' ability to read with ease and confidence. It contains 15 mini-books on topics from core curricular areas, tied in with national standards at the third-grade level and presented as fiction, nonfiction, poetry, and prose. It also offers tools for assessment, including a teacher checklist and rubric and a checklist students can use to monitor their own reading progress. (See Assessing Fluency, page 9.)

The mini-books and accompanying activities target specific skills in fluency and phonics and aim to increase speed of word recognition as well as to improve decoding accuracy, use of expression, and, ultimately, comprehension. The text adheres to vocabulary standards based on the studies of Harris and Jacobson. These standards ensure that your students will encounter words within the first-grade reading vocabulary rather than those that might hinder their progress.

The stories have been leveled using readability scores from the Lexile Framework for Reading (See chart, page 14.) These scores offer guidelines to help you select the stories that best match the needs and reading levels of each student. The stories are ready for use to practice, strengthen, and assess skills in reading fluency. And they all share the same objective: to give students practice reading comfortably, confidently, and with enthusiasm, so that you can build an ever-growing flock of fluent readers within the walls of your classroom.

# Fluency: An Overview

## What Is Fluency?

Fluency is the mark of a proficient reader. When a student reads text quickly, gets most of the words right, and uses appropriate expression and phrasing, we say that he or she has achieved fluency. Fluency frees readers from the struggle that slows them down. Hence, they are able to read for meaning and to understand. They can attend to the details of text, pausing as indicated and varying tone and pace to enhance comprehension for both themselves and potential listeners.

## How Does Fluency Develop?

As with every skill worth developing, fluency sharpens with experience. Exposure to print, immersion in a rich linguistic environment, and practice, practice, practice all lead to fluent reading.

From the emergent on up, readers must learn and apply tools to help them advance. The National Institute for Literacy (NIFL) speaks of fluency as a skill in flux.

> "Fluency is not a stage of development at which readers can read all words quickly and easily. Fluency changes, depending on what readers are reading, their familiarity with the words, and the amount of their practice with reading text. Even very skilled readers may read in a slow, labored manner when reading texts with many unfamiliar words or topics." (NIFL, 2001)

Readers are most comfortable (and most fluent) when reading what they have seen before or what they know most about. When venturing beyond that, they must rely on word attack skills, prior knowledge, and the host of tools that helped them advance previously.

"Fluent readers read aloud effortlessly and with expression. Their reading sounds natural, as if they are speaking. Readers who have not yet developed fluency read slowly, word by word. Their oral reading is choppy and plodding."

NATIONAL INSTITUTE FOR LITERACY, 2001

# Ways to Build Fluency

Two words encompass what readers require for the development of fluency: *exposure* and *practice*. To foster fluent reading, be sure to:

* **MODEL FLUENT READING.** Read aloud to students. As you read, model (and point out) aspects of fluent reading such as phrasing, pacing, and expression. Help students understand that people aren't born knowing how to do this; they learn it by hearing it and trying it themselves.

* **PROVIDE STUDENTS WITH PLENTY OF READING PRACTICE.** Oral reading is highly effective for tracking and strengthening fluency. It enables both the reader and the listener to hear the reader and assess progress, and it allows the listener to provide guidance as needed. Whisper reading serves as a transition from oral to silent reading. In whisper reading, all students read aloud at the same time, but at a volume that is just barely audible. The student is able to self-monitor and the teacher to move around the room, noting progress, keeping students on task, and offering guidance as needed. For silent reading, students read an assigned passage or a book of their own choice. Because the reader cannot be heard, assessment of reading skill is not possible. The value of silent reading is that it increases time spent reading and gives students "opportunities to expand and practice reading strategies." (Fountas and Pinnell, 2001)

* **SELECT APPROPRIATE TEXT.** To develop fluency, a student must practice reading text at his or her independent reading level—the level at which he or she is able to accurately decode 96 to 100 percent of the words in a given text. This level varies for every student. By assessing each student's reading level up front, you will be prepared to select appropriate texts and ensure that your students get a lot of practice reading at a level at which they achieve success. (Rasinski, 2003; Worthy and Broaddus, 2001/2002) For information about how to use text to assess fluency, see Assessing Fluency, page 9.

* **RAISE THE BAR.** Read aloud to students from text that is above their independent reading level, exposing them to new and more difficult words and concepts without the pressure of having to decode.

* **GIVE ROOM TO GROW.** To help a student advance in fluency, present text at his or her instructional level. This text can be read with 90 to 95 percent accuracy. With a little help, the student can get almost all the words right. (Blevins, 2001a; Rasinski, 2003)

* **PROVIDE DIRECT INSTRUCTION AND FEEDBACK.** Prepare students before they read. First, review phonics skills they will need to decode words. Draw attention to sight words, root words, affixes, and word chunks. Pre-teach difficult or unfamiliar words. Demonstrate the use of intonation, phrasing, and expression, and tell children when they have done these well. Listen to children read, and offer praise as well as helpful tips for the next attempt.

---

> "Fluency develops when children do lots of reading and writing—including lots of easy text. Repeated reading helps children develop fluency because with each reading their word identification becomes quicker and more automatic, freeing attention for expression, phrasing, and comprehension."
>
> (CUNNINGHAM, 2005)

✳ **USE A VARIETY OF READING MATERIALS.** Plays, fiction stories, nonfiction passages, and poetry offer a rich and varied reading experience. Expose your students to each of these. Give them many opportunities to get excited about and immerse themselves in what they are reading.

✳ **HIGHLIGHT PHRASING.** One of the most effective ways to help students who are struggling with fluency is to use phrase-cued text. Phrase-cued text is marked by slashes to indicate where readers should pause. One slash indicates a pause or a meaningful chunk of text within a sentence. Two slashes indicate a longer pause at the end of a sentence. Ready-made samples of phrase-cued text are available (see Resources for Reading Fluency and Comprehension, page 19), but you can also convert any passage of text to phrase-cued text by reading it aloud, listening for pauses and meaningful chunks of text, and drawing slashes in the appropriate places. (See the example, right, from the mini-book "How Do Animals Sleep?," page 37.) Model fluent reading with proper phrasing, and invite students to practice with the text you have marked.

*Phrase Cued s*

### How Do Animals Sleep?

Inside?// Outside?// Upside down?//
Where/ and how/ do animals sleep?//

Lights out!// Bats sleep/ in dark places,/ such as caves.// Bats hang/ upside down/ while sleeping.// They hold themselves/ in place/ with strong claws.//

Treetops/ are tempting!// Birds make nests/ in trees/ and sleep there.// Sometimes,/ birds sleep on branches.// A sleeping bird/ holds a branch tightly/ with its feet.//

> "Students who are having trouble with comprehension may not be putting words together in meaningful phrases or chunks as they read. Their oral reading is characterized by a choppy, word-by-word delivery that impedes comprehension. These students need instruction in phrasing written text into appropriate segments."
>
> (BLEVINS, 2001A)

## Bringing Oral Reading Into Your Classroom

Provide opportunities for children to read aloud. This may include all or any of the following:

✳ **INTERACTIVE READ-ALOUD:** An adult reader demonstrates fluent oral reading and talks about how he or she changes tone, pace, or expression in response to the story. Students enjoy a dramatic reading and absorb skills in fluent reading. In addition, the interactive read-aloud provides an opportunity for teachers to ask open-ended questions before, during, and after the reading, soliciting students' prior knowledge and extending their understanding, comprehension, and connection with the topic. This connection can advance student interaction with the text and promote optimal conditions for fluency.

✳ **SHARED READING:** An adult reader models fluent reading and then invites children to read along, using big books or small-group instruction.

> As the child approaches a new text he is entitled to an introduction so that when he reads, the gist of the whole or partly revealed story can provide some guide for a fluent reading. He will understand what he reads if it refers to things he knows about, or has read about previously, so that he is familiar with the topic, the vocabulary or the story itself.

(CLAY, 1991)

* **CHORAL READING:** An adult and children read aloud together. This activity works especially well with poetry and cumulative tales.

* **ECHO READING:** A child repeats phrases or sentences read by someone else, mimicking tone, expression, and pacing.

* **REPEATED READING:** An adult reads aloud while a student listens and reads again while the student follows along. Then the adult invites the student to read along, and, finally, the student reads the same text aloud alone. This technique is most helpful for struggling readers.

* **PAIRED REPEATED READING:** Teachers group students in pairs, matching above-level readers with on-level readers and on-level readers with those below level. Partners are encouraged to take turns reading aloud to each other, each reading a short passage three times and then getting feedback. The manner of grouping provides every struggling reader with a more proficient reader to model.

* **READERS' THEATER:** Students work in groups to rehearse and perform a brief play before the class. Performing can be exciting, and the drive to present well can be a powerful force behind mastering fluency in reading and speech, motivating both struggling and proficient readers.

* **TAPE-ASSISTED READING:** Children listen to books-on-tape while reading along in a book. (Consider recording your own tapes if commercially made tapes go too quickly, or if the tapes include background elements such as music or sound effects, which can be distracting.) Children can also listen and critique their own reading on tape.

* **PHRASE-CUED TEXT:** (See Highlight Phrasing, page 7.)

## Where Does Vocabulary Fit In?

Stumbling over the words constitutes one of the main setbacks on the way to fluency. It remains in your students' best interest, then, to grow familiar with words they will likely encounter in reading. Cunningham and Allington (2003) urge active use of word walls, inviting student participation in choosing words to put on the walls, eliminating words hardly used, and reviewing the list words daily.

## Enhancing Comprehension

In all reading instruction, it is important to remember that reading imparts meaning, and so the fundamental goal of reading is to comprehend. All other instruction—phonics, phonemic awareness, auditory discrimination—is wasted effort if comprehension gets lost in the process. Consequently, those who find no purpose or meaning in the written word will soon lose interest in reading altogether.

Avoid this by teaching your students strategies to enhance comprehension. Help them learn to question the text they are reading. *What is the message?*

*Does it make sense to them? Do they know what it means?* Find out by asking questions. Ask questions before students read, to prepare them for the story. Ask as they read, to deepen their understanding of the text. Ask additional questions after they read, to clear up any comprehension issues and summarize the story. Teach your students to formulate questions of their own to give them a vested interest in what they are reading.

# Assessing Fluency

There are two ways to assess a student's progress in fluency: informally and formally. Informal assessment involves listening to students read aloud, noting how easily, quickly, and accurately they read and deciding how well they attend to phrasing, expression, and other elements. Formal assessment involves timing a student's oral reading to create a tangible record of his or her progress throughout the school year.

To conduct an informal assessment of students' reading fluency, use the reproducible Teacher Checklist and Rubric for Oral Reading Fluency, on page 10. Have a student read aloud for five to seven minutes while you note on the form the strategies the student uses as well as his or her reading strengths and difficulties.

Students can monitor their own progress using the Student Checklist for Self-Assessment, on page 11. Photocopy and laminate one for each student. Review the checklist components with students many times, until they understand the purpose of the checklist and the meaning of each sentence. Encourage students to mentally complete the checklist from time to time to track their own reading fluency.

To carry out timed repeated reading, select a passage of text (150–250 words) that is at the student's independent reading level and that he or she has never read before. Have the student read aloud the passage for one minute. Track your own copy of the text while he or she reads, marking words omitted or pronounced incorrectly. Count the number of words the student read correctly. Then give the student three one-minute opportunities (in separate sessions) to read the same text, and average the scores to obtain his or her oral reading fluency rate.*

## ❧ In Conclusion

Does fluency instruction work? Research has shown that concentrated reading instruction can dramatically improve reading comprehension and fluency, which in turn affect academic performance, self-esteem, and overall achievement. With this in mind, it is not only helpful to instruct with an eye toward fluency, it is essential.

---

* For more detailed information on timed reading, consult Blevins (2001a, pp. 9–12) and Rasinski (2003, pp. 82–83).

> "Instruction that focuses too heavily on word-perfect decoding sends a message that good reading is nothing more than accurate word recognition. As a result, students tend to shoot for accuracy at the expense of everything else, including meaning."
>
> (RASINSKI, 2004)

> "The majority of children who enter kindergarten and elementary school at risk for reading failure can learn to read at average or above-average levels—if they are identified early and given systematic, intensive instruction in phonemic awareness, phonics, reading fluency, vocabulary, and reading comprehension strategies."
>
> (LYON AND CHHABRA, 2004; ORIGINALLY CREDITED TO LYON ET AL., 2001 AND TORGESEN, 2002)

Child's Name: _____ Date: _____

Grade: _____ Passage: _____

# Teacher Checklist and Rubric for Oral Reading Fluency

## Oral Reading Checklist

| The reader: | Usually | Sometimes | Seldom |
|---|---|---|---|
| self-corrects as he or she reads. ................................. | _____ | _____ | _____ |
| attempts to read/pronounce unfamiliar words. ........................... | _____ | _____ | _____ |
| reads in meaningful phrases or word chunks. ............................ | _____ | _____ | _____ |
| reads smoothly without frequent pauses. ............................... | _____ | _____ | _____ |
| attends to punctuation at the end of a sentence. ........................ | _____ | _____ | _____ |
| reads with appropriate expression. ................................. | _____ | _____ | _____ |

## Oral Reading Rubric

**4**  The child reads in meaningful phrases. The child responds to punctuation through appropriate pausing and intonation. The child usually self-corrects while reading. The child reads with expression and works to pronounce unfamiliar words, repeating them if necessary to ensure accuracy.

**3**  The child reads primarily in meaningful phrases. The child attends to most punctuation and usually reads at a smooth pace, but sometimes struggles with words or sentence structure. The child often self-corrects but does not always recognize errors. The child reads with expression and attempts to pronounce unfamiliar words, but sometimes needs assistance.

**2**  The child reads primarily in groups of two or three words. The child reads smoothly at times and then slowly, word by word, especially when encountering unfamiliar words. The child pays little attention to punctuation, pacing, and expression and spends most of the effort on decoding. The child hesitates before trying new words and usually requires assistance with them.

**1**  The child reads slowly and word by word. The child does not heed punctuation and reads words in a string without pause or expression. The child does not attempt to pronounce unfamiliar words. The child's reading sounds stilted and unnatural and lacks meaning.

Adapted from *35 Rubrics & Checklists to Assess Reading and Writing* by Adele Fiderer. Scholastic, 1998. Permission to reuse granted by the author.

Name: _____

# My Read-Aloud Checklist

|  |  | Yes | Sometimes | No |
|---|---|---|---|---|
| **1** | I say a word again if it does not sound right. | ☐ | ☐ | ☐ |
| **2** | I pay attention to punctuation at the end of a sentence. | ☐ | ☐ | ☐ |
| **3** | I try to read without stopping after every word. | ☐ | ☐ | ☐ |
| **4** | I read with expression. | ☐ | ☐ | ☐ |
| **5** | I look at the pictures to see what is happening. | ☐ | ☐ | ☐ |

Adapted from *35 Rubrics & Checklists to Assess Reading and Writing* by Adele Fiderer. Scholastic, 1998. Permission to reuse granted by the author.

*Fluency Practice Mini-Books: Grade 3*   Scholastic Teaching Resources

# Using the Mini-Books to Enhance Fluency

## A Fluency Mini-Lesson

Use this sample mini-lesson as a model for using the mini-books to strengthen and assess students' reading fluency.

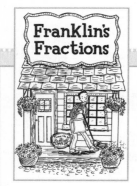

**MINI-BOOK 2**

### Franklin's Fractions

**PREPARATION:** Give each student a copy of the mini-book "Franklin's Fractions" (pages 25–28). Help students assemble the books, or construct them in advance. (See How to Make the Mini-Books, page 18.)

## Pre-Reading

**1.** Introduce unfamiliar or difficult words that students will come across in the text. These might include *Franklin, Walter William, fractions, three-quarter, slices, one-third, separately,* and *notice* as well as some of the sight words: *idea's* and *might*. Help students decode the words. Review them several times to aid recognition and boost fluency. (See Preparing for Difficult or Unfamiliar Text, page 15, for more about the vocabulary in the mini-books.)

**2.** Review reading techniques that promote fluency, such as reading from left to right, "smooshing" words together to sound like talking, and crossing the page with a steady, sweeping eye movement. (Blevins, 2001a)

## Reading and Modeling

**1.** Depending on students' level of reading proficiency, you may want to read aloud the story first and then invite them to read along with you in their mini-books. As you read, point out ways in which your pacing, intonation, and expression lend meaning to the text. You might say:

> "Listen while I reread the words 'Come on in!' What did I do with my voice to make those words sound cheerful? What did I see in the sentence that told me to do that?" (*exclamation point*)

or

> "Did you notice how my voice rose at the end of the sentence 'Notice how it's cut in two?' That's what we do when we see a question mark. We know the sentence is asking something; we use our voices to make it sound that way."

Walter William Franklin hung a sign outside his door. "Come on in!" the sign said. "I sell fractions in my store!"

①

"How can you sell fractions?" people asked. "How can it be?" "I sell things in parts," said Walter William. "Come and see."

②

"Want a three-quarter pizza?
Let me turn the oven on. This one
had eight slices. See? Now two
of them are gone."

③

"Here I have a cupcake.
Notice how it's cut in two?
I'll sell each half separately.
That is what I do."

④

"I am selling lemonade
for less. Now, have you heard?
Three cups for one dollar
means that one cup is one-third!"

⑤

"I give change in fractions, too,"
said Walter William. "See? If you
pay four quarters, you might get
one back from me."

⑥

"Franklin's Fractions!" people said.
"The idea's rather nice! Now you
need to run a sale and offer things
half-price!"

⑦

**2.** Try reading the sentences without the inflection. Point out that questions read without the appropriate tone sound flat and stilted, without depth, character, or expression.

**3.** Read the story aloud again, inviting students to read aloud with you as they are able. NOTE: If you feel that a group of readers is already proficient, preview the words and then have children read the story aloud without modeling.

**4.** Once readers have read the story several times, go back and emphasize aspects of phonics and vocabulary that will increase their understanding of language; encourage faster, more accurate reading; and deepen comprehension. (You may want to write the story on sentence strips and use a pocket chart to manipulate words and phrases.) "Franklin's Fractions" presents opportunities to explore such topics as:

* **rhyming:** *door, store; heard, third; nice, price*. Have students underline the rhyming words in each verse.

* **quantitative words:** *three-quarter, two, eight, half, one dollar, half-price, one-third, quarters*. Have students put a dot under all the number words in the mini-book.

* **phrasing:** Readers must pause after all ending punctuation. They will pause ever so briefly after each comma, as in the sentence "If you pay four quarters, you might get one back from me."

* **dialogue:** Help readers practice using clues in punctuation, text placement, and vocabulary to determine who is speaking and when. Point out that each time a character speaks, the words that he or she says are contained within quotation marks. An indented paragraph indicates that a new speaker is talking. Dialogue words such as "said" and "cried" highlight who is speaking.

**5.** The methods described here feature shared reading and Reader's Theater. Other options for use with this mini-book include timed reading for assessment of each child's rate of fluency, paired repeated reading, and choral reading.

Fluency techniques such as echo reading work well with stories containing repetitive or rhythmic text, which naturally lead the reader to pause in the middle of a sentence rather than strictly at the end. This method gives students the opportunity to step in and participate in the oral reading. "Under the Bridge," page 33, and "The Other Side of the Sea," page 41, offer examples of such text.

# Mini-Book Readability Scores

The chart below shows the readability scores of the stories in this collection. The texts were leveled using the Lexile Framework for Reading. These scores offer guidelines to help you select the stories that best match the needs and reading levels of each student. For more information about the Lexile Framework, go to www.lexile.com. (See Preparing for Difficult or Unfamiliar Text, page 15, for more about the vocabulary in the mini-books.)

| Story Title | Lexile Score |
| --- | --- |
| 1.  Meeting George Washington | 350L |
| 2.  Franklin's Fractions | 360L |
| 3.  What Simple Machines Are These? | 380L |
| 4.  Under the Bridge | 420L |
| 5.  How Do Animals Sleep? | 470L |
| 6.  The Other Side of the Sea | 480L |
| 7.  The Man, the Boy, and the Donkey | 500L |
| 8.  The Day the Sun Didn't Shine | 500L |
| 9.  What's the Matter? | 510L |
| 10.  Pass the Chips! | 530L |
| 11.  Tornado! | 540L |
| 12.  Man on the Moon | 540L |
| 13.  Born to Fly | 550L |
| 14.  A View From the Top | 550L |
| 15.  Sal Fink | 550L |

A Lexile Score of **350 to 550** is appropriate for the third-grade independent reading level.

# Preparing for Difficult or Unfamiliar Text

To assess fluency, have children read text that is new to them. (Blevins, 2001a) With this in mind, when using the mini-books for assessment, do not prepare students by introducing unfamiliar or difficult words. Pre-reading may distort the assessment results.

Before reading for the purpose of developing fluency, however, it is helpful to highlight words that may prove to be stumbling blocks for young or struggling readers. Words slightly above grade level, difficult words on grade level, and complex high-frequency words can be daunting when encountered for the first time within text. To prevent this, introduce words and help children decode them before they read. Give them a chance to decipher the words before you provide correct pronunciation. Then review the words several times to aid recognition and boost fluency.

The words listed below may be unfamiliar or challenging to your students. Some are within the common third grade vocabulary but may contain difficult or unfamiliar letter patterns. Others have been categorized as common to text read by slightly older readers. (Harris and Jacobson, 1982) These words were selected for use in the mini-books when necessary to enhance the flow of the text or where substitutions would not carry the same meaning, such as the words *inclined* and *pulley* in "What Simple Machines Are These?," page 29. Note that proper nouns are excluded from leveling.

**Meeting George Washington**
*George Washington, dizzy, general, impatient, Delaware River, British, soldiers*

**Franklin's Fractions**
*Walter William Franklin, fractions, three-quarter, slices, one-third*

**What Simple Machines Are These?**
*attention, Mr. Barlow, clues, simple, Jules, Carlos, Marla, stroller, ramp, inclined, pulleys, lever*

**Under the Bridge**
*meadow, wooden, troll, waded, lonely*

**How Do Animals Sleep?**
*claws, tempting, bunches, fluffy*

**The Other Side of the Sea**
*America, sprays, uneasy, symbol, freedom, Statue, Liberty, graceful, Ellis Island*

**The Man, the Boy, and the Donkey**
*switched, village, selfish, shame*

**The Day the Sun Didn't Shine**
*complained, hedgehog, headache, sliver, moonlight, shone, snorted, impossible, huddled, petals, glared, remarked*

**What's the Matter?**
*Professor, tuna, students, Michelle, Shiro, Tori, bonus, solid, liquid, boils, steam, vapor, temperature, challenge*

**Pass the Chips!**
*restaurant, chef, batch, Saratoga Chips, Saratoga Springs, menu*

**Tornado!**
*tornado, Oklahoma, trailers, destroys, underground, littered, tractors*

**Man on the Moon**
*astronauts, Columbia, Eagle, Michael Collins, Neil Armstrong, Buzz Aldrin, mankind, collected, soil, samples, heroes, American*

**Born to Fly**
*Amelia Earhart, Canary, flight, license, received, phone, Captain H. H. Railey, Atlantic, passenger, Hawaii, Washington, sixty-six, courage, skill*

**A View From the Top**
*Meg Lowman, treetops, rainforest, scientist, affect, steel, harness, sting, poison, thorny, collects*

**Sal Fink**
*Mike Fink, riverboat, Mississippi, Ohio, roughest, toughest, Sal Fink, alligators, upstream, wrestled, pirates, coyote*

# Activities for Building Fluency

## ● Attend to Punctuation

Emphasize the impact of ending punctuation. Model and then invite students to say the same sentence three different ways, using a period, a question mark, and an exclamation point. For example, from "What's the Matter?," page 53, you might read the sentence "You solved my bonus questions!" as follows:

&#10033; "You solved my bonus questions."

&#10033; "You solved my bonus questions?"

&#10033; "You solved my bonus questions!"

## ● Explore Dialogue

Use a mini-book filled with conversation, such as "What Simple Machines Are These?," page 29, or "The Man, the Boy, and the Donkey," page 45, to draw attention to using dialogue to represent each character's unique personality. For example, when reading aloud "What Simple Machines Are These?," purposely model distinct voices for Mr. Barlow, Jules, Carlos, and Marla. Discuss the ways you change inflection, accent, pace, and tone to represent each character. When Mr. Barlow speaks, for example, you may want to talk slowly and carefully. For Marla, you may choose to speak more quickly and in a higher-pitched voice. Each person's speech will hold its own distinct sound; repeat it each time that character speaks. Point out your intentions to your students, and encourage them to create their own unique voices for characters—in this mini-book and in trade books they read aloud.

In addition, use oral reading to demonstrate the ways speech can reflect emotion. The dialogue in "The Man, the Boy, and the Donkey," provides a particularly good opportunity for this; the scorn and criticism of the passersby can be conveyed through pitch (how high or low), tone (nature of expression), and pace (degree of speed) throughout the story, ending with the old man's quiet wisdom.

## Connect With Phonics

Each mini-book offers opportunities to extend phonics awareness. While reading, look for connections to the following:

### Letter-Sound Relationships

* blends and digraphs
* high-frequency words
* vowel sounds
* word families
* rhyme

### Word Structure

* compound words
* contractions
* homonyms
* plurals
* prefixes and suffixes
* syllabication

## Identify Key Text Features With Highlighting Tape

Use colorful highlighting tape to flag words previously introduced as well as to mark the beginning and end of text children will be expected to read. Students can also use highlighting tape to emphasize repetitive phrases, rhyming words, sight words, and word chunks, as well as to mark dialogue for Readers' Theater.

## Reinforce Understanding With a Pocket Chart

Use a pocket chart to reinforce pacing, intonation, chunking, and other aspects of fluent reading. Focus on one mini-book and one skill at a time. For example, to guide children in reading smoothly instead of word by word, determine where natural phrasing groups words together, such as "The man walked" in the sentence "The man walked while his son rode" (from the mini-book "The Man, the Boy, and the Donkey," page 45). Write each word on its own strip, and place these words in order on the chart. Read aloud the words, separately at first, and then blending, or "smooshing," them together. (Blevins, 2001a) Next, substitute the individual words for a larger strip featuring the words in a group rather than individually. (Example: "The man walked" would be a natural word group.)

Invite children to manipulate sentences on the pocket chart, writing whole sentences on strips and then cutting them apart to show natural groupings.

# How to Make the Mini-Books

1. Remove the mini-book pages to be copied, tearing along the perforation.

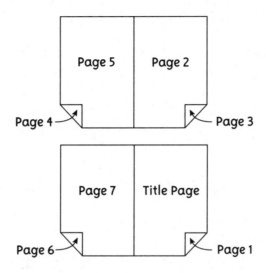

2. For each book, make a double-sided copy of the pages on 8 1/2- by 11-inch copy paper.

3. Once you have double-sided copies of the pages, place page 2 behind the title page.

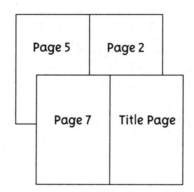

4. Fold the pages in half along the solid line.

5. Check to be sure that the pages are in proper order, and then staple them together along the book's spine.

- If your machine does not have a double-sided function, make copies of the title page and page 7 first. Place this copy in the machine's paper tray. Then make a test copy of the second page (pages 1 and 6) to be sure that it copies onto the back of the title page and page 7.

- Alternatively, you can simple photocopy single-sided copies of each page, cut apart the mini-book pages, and stack them together in order, with the title page on top. Then staple the pages together along the book's spine.

# Resources for Reading Fluency and Comprehension

Armbruster, Bonnie B., Ph.D., Fran Lehr, M.A., and Jean Osborn, M.Ed., *A Child Becomes a Reader.* (RMC Research Corporation/Partnership for Reading: National Institute for Literacy, National Institute of Child Health and Human Development, U.S. Department of Education, and U.S. Department of Health and Human Services, 2003).

Beck, Isabel L., Margaret G. McKeown, and Linda Kucan. *Bringing Words to Life: Robust Vocabulary Instruction.* New York: The Guilford Press, 2002.

Blevins, Wiley. *Building Fluency: Lessons and Strategies for Reading Success.* New York: Scholastic, 2001a.*

Blevins, Wiley. *Teaching Phonics and Word Study.* New York: Scholastic, 2001b.

Clay, Marie M. *Becoming Literate: The Construction of Inner Control.* Portsmouth, NH: Heinemann, 1991.

Cunningham, Patricia M., *Phonics They Use: Words for Reading and Writing.* Boston: Pearson Education, Inc., 2005.

Cunningham, Patricia M., and Richard L. Allington. *Classrooms That Work: They Can ALL Read and Write.* New York: Pearson Education, 2003.

Cunningham, Patricia M., Dorothy P. Hall, and Cheryl M. Sigmon. *The Teacher's Guide to the Four Blocks.* Greensboro, NC: Carson-Dellosa, 1999.

Fiderer, Adele. *40 Rubrics & Checklists to Assess Reading and Writing.* New York: Scholastic, 1999.

Fiderer, Adele. *35 Rubrics & Checklists to Assess Reading and Writing.* New York: Scholastic, 1998.

*Fluency Formula: Grades 1–6.* New York: Scholastic, 2003.*

Fountas, Irene C., and Gay Su Pinnell. *Guiding Readers and Writers (Grades 3–6): Teaching Comprehension, Genre, and Content Literacy.* Portsmouth, NH: Heinemann, 2001.

Fresch, Mary Jo, and Aileen Wheaton. *Teaching and Assessing Spelling.* New York: Scholastic, 2002.

Harris, A. J., and M. D. Jacobson. *Basic Reading Vocabularies.* New York: Macmillan, 1982.

Heilman, Arthur W. *Phonics in Perspective.* Upper Saddle River, NJ: Pearson Education, 2002.

Kieff, Judith. "Revisiting the Read-Aloud." *Childhood Education*. Volume 80, No. 1, p. 28.

Lyon, G. R., J. M. Fletcher, S. E. Shaywitz, B. A. Shaywitz, J. K. Torgesen, F. B. Wood, A. Shulte, and R. Olson. "Rethinking Learning Disabilities." In C. E. Finn, R. A. J. Rotherham, and C. R. Hokanson (Eds.), *Rethinking Special Education for a New Century*. Washington, D.C.: Thomas B. Fordham Foundation & Progressive Policy Institute, 2001, pp. 259–287.

Lyon, G. Reid. "Why Reading Is Not a Natural Process." *Educational Leadership*, Volume 55, No. 6 (March 1998): pp. 14–18.

Lyon, G. Reid, and Vinita Chhabra. "The Science of Reading Research." *Educational Leadership*, Volume 61, No. 6 (March 2004): pp. 12–17.

Pennington, Mark. *Better Spelling in 5 Minutes a Day*. Roseville, CA: Prima Publishing, 2001.

Pinnell, Gay Su, and Patricia L. Scharer. *Teaching for Comprehension in Reading*. New York: Scholastic, 2003.*

Rasinski, Timothy. "Creating Fluent Readers." *Educational Leadership*, Volume 61, No. 6 (March 2004): pp. 46–51.

Rasinski, Timothy V. *The Fluent Reader*. New York: Scholastic, 2003.*

Tomlinson, Carol Ann. *The Differentiated Classroom*. Alexandria, VA: ASCD, 1999.

Torgesen, J. K. "The Prevention of Reading Difficulties." *Journal of School Psychology*, Volume 40, Issue 1, pp. 7–26.

Wagstaff, Janiel M. *Teaching Reading and Writing With Word Walls*. New York: Scholastic, 1999.

White, Sheida. "Listening to Children Read Aloud: Oral Fluency." *NAEP Facts*, National Center for Education Statistics. Volume 1, Number 1.

Worthy, Jo, and Karen Broaddus. "Fluency Beyond the Primary Grades: From Group Performance to Silent, Independent Reading." *The Reading Teacher*, Volume 55, No. 4, (December 2001/January 2002): pp. 334–343.

Worthy, Jo, and Kathryn Prater. "I Thought About It All Night: Readers Theatre for Reading Fluency and Motivation (The Intermediate Grades)." *The Reading Teacher*, Volume 56, No. 3 (November 2002): p. 294.

Yopp, Hallie Kay, and Ruth Helen Yopp. "Supporting Phonemic Awareness Development in the Classroom." *The Reading Teacher*, Volume 54, No. 2 (October 2000): pp. 130–143.

* This resource includes samples and/or examples of phrase-cued text.

# Meeting George Washington

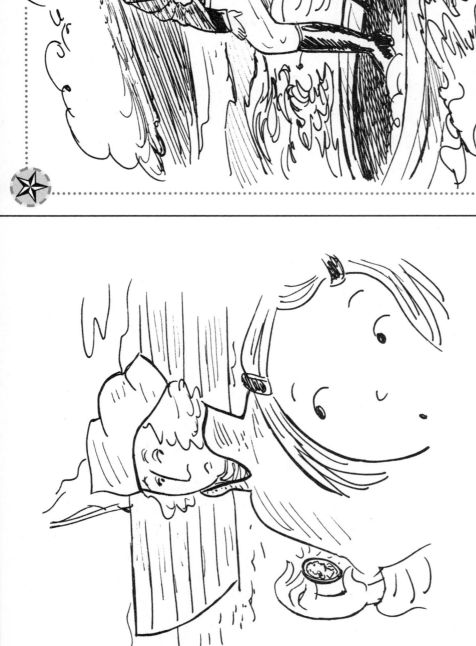

Kerry felt cold, small, and afraid. "I'm not a soldier," she said. "I'm just a girl who needs to go home." Kerry looked at the quarter again. George Washington's face appeared. What do you think will happen next?

One day, Kerry sat in her bedroom and counted her money. One quarter looked more shiny than the rest. Kerry picked it up. She looked at the face on it. "That's George Washington," said Kerry.

"Where is this boat going?" asked Kerry. George Washington looked impatient. "We're crossing the Delaware River to get to the British soldiers. We want to take them by surprise."

All at once, Kerry felt a strange wind wrap around her. She felt dizzy and cold. "Step on the boat, please," a voice said.

Kerry held up the quarter. It was just a piece of metal. George's face was gone! "Please step on the boat so we can get going," said George Washington.

Kerry looked up. She was not in her bedroom now. Instead, she stood in the snow at the edge of a river. A tall man in a long cape stood before her.

"You're George Washington!" exclaimed Kerry. "Your face is on my quarter!"

"I am George Washington," replied the general. "But what is a quarter?"

# Franklin's Fractions

"Franklin's Fractions!" people said.

"The idea's rather nice! Now you

need to run a sale and offer things

half-price!"

Walter William Franklin hung a sign outside his door.

"Come on in!" the sign said.

"I sell fractions in my store!"

"I give change in fractions, too," said Walter William. "See? If you pay four quarters, you might get one back from me."

"How can you sell fractions?"
people asked. "How can it be?"
"I sell things in parts," said Walter
William. "Come and see."

"I am selling lemonade
for less. Now, have you heard?
Three cups for one dollar means
that one cup is one-third!"

"Want a three-quarter pizza?
Let me turn the oven on. This one
had eight slices. See? Now two
of them are gone."

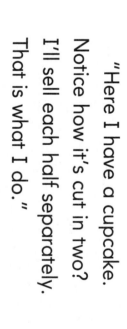

"Here I have a cupcake.
Notice how it's cut in two?
I'll sell each half separately.
That is what I do."

# What Simple Machines Are These?

Simple Machines

inclined plane | pulley | lever
ramp | crane | seesaw
slide | clothesline | crowbar

"A seesaw is a lever!" cried Carlos.

"You've guessed them all!" said Mr. Barlow.

"Now, what did you learn?"

"Simple machines make work easier!"
said Jules. "And they're all around us!"

7

"Attention, class!" said Mr. Barlow. He handed out a page of clues. "I'd like you to figure out what simple machines these are."

Jules, Carlos, and Marla worked together.

"Here's the first clue," read Carlos.

 1

---

"Sit upon a seesaw.
Choose an end. Just one!
You'll go up when I sit down.
I'll lift you for fun!"

6

"People use pulleys to help them lift things," said Jules. "Pulleys make the job easier."

Marla read the next clue.

"This will help you move a load without lifting it. Push a stroller up a ramp. You won't need to quit."

SIMPLE MACHINES

inclined plane

"A ramp is an inclined plane!" said Marla.
She wrote "inclined plane" on the line beside the clue.
"Okay," said Jules. "Here's the next clue."

"Have a heavy pail to lift?
Tie it to a rope.
Pull the rope over a wheel.
Easy lift, I hope!"

# Under the Bridge

"We don't care if you're clean or neat.
Just being nice would be a treat."
And so the troll came out that day.
He made new friends and learned to play.

7

In a field of sweet green grass there lived three goats. Their meadow lay at the edge of a great wooden bridge. Under the bridge lived a mean and muddy troll.

The goats trotted all the way across the bridge. Then they turned around and waded through the water. There they found the troll. He looked sad and lonely.

One day, the three goats tried to cross
the bridge. As soon as they stepped on it,
the troll called out in a loud, mean voice.
"This bridge is mine. I am the boss!
Stay off my bridge. You may not cross!"

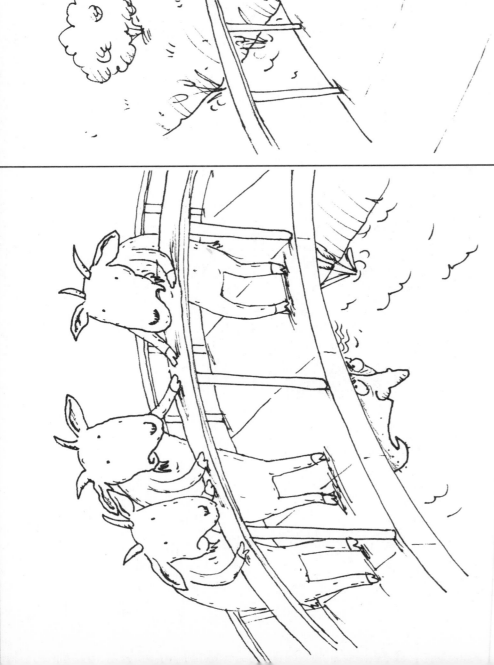

After a long silence, the troll spoke.
"I cannot come up there, you see.
I don't want you to look at me.
I don't take baths. I'm on my own.
I'm muddy, mean, and all alone."

The goats stood still and called out. "This little bridge is ours to use. We'll walk across it if we choose."

The troll spoke in a louder, meaner voice. "Stay off my bridge! Get off, I say, or I will make you run away!"

The goats walked to the center of the bridge. Again, they called to the troll. "Come up on top and let us see who won't let us walk happily."

# How Do Animals Sleep?

What about life underground?

Foxes sleep in underground dens.
A sleepy fox curls up and uses its
fluffy tail for a pillow.

These are some ways in which animals
sleep. What other ways have you seen?

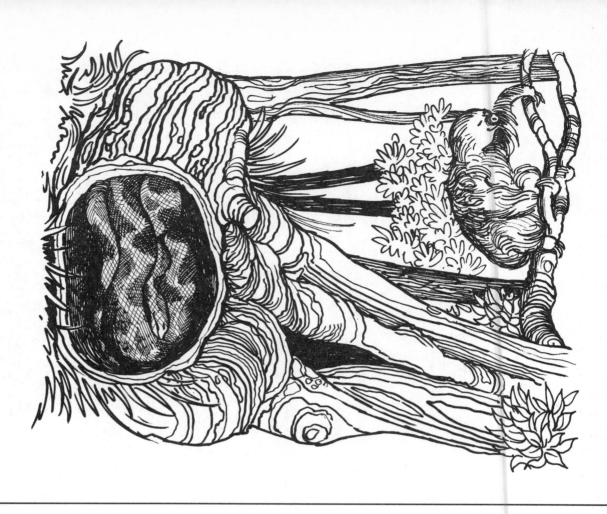

Inside? Outside? Upside down?
Where and how do animals sleep?

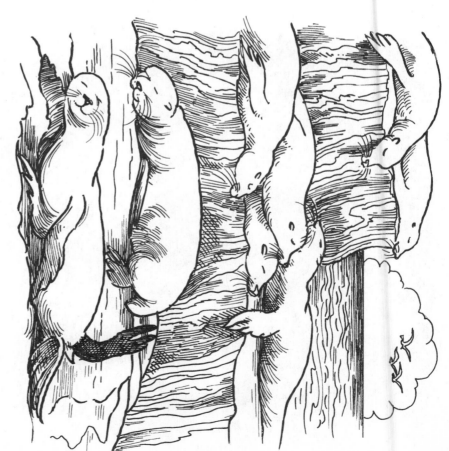

Sea lions sleep in and out of the water.
When they sleep in the ocean, only their
noses stick out of the water. The rest
of their bodies hang down. Sea lions
sleep on land, too. They take group naps
on large rocks.

Lights out! Bats sleep in dark places, such as caves. Bats hang upside down while sleeping. They hold themselves in place with strong claws.

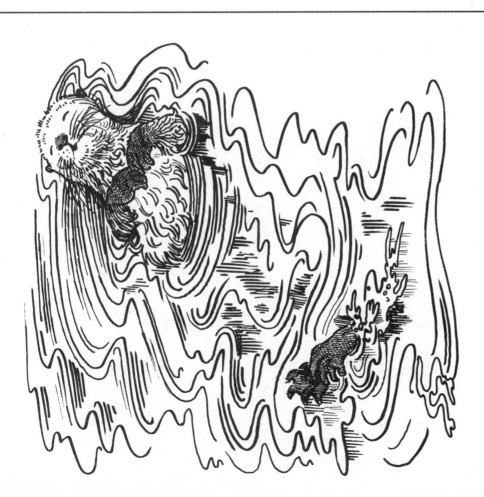

How about a real waterbed? Sea otters float on their backs while they nap. First, they wind seaweed around their feet. This keeps the otters from floating away.

5

Treetops are tempting! Birds make nests in trees and sleep there. Sometimes, birds sleep on branches. A sleeping bird holds a branch tightly with its feet.

Even big animals sleep in trees. Monkeys lie on branches or bunches of leaves. Monkeys wrap their tails around the branches. This keeps the monkeys from falling while they sleep.

# The ❖ Other Side of the Sea

We step off the boat
onto a new shore.
We've reached Ellis Island,
America's door.

7

We stand on the deck
with our backs to the sea:
my mother, my father,
my brother, and me.

"Welcome!"
the lady in robes seems to say.
Our eyes fill with tears.
We have come a long way.

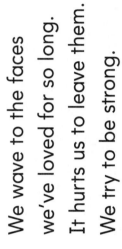

We wave to the faces
we've loved for so long.
It hurts us to leave them.
We try to be strong.

Then we see a symbol
of freedom for all.
The Statue of Liberty,
graceful and tall.

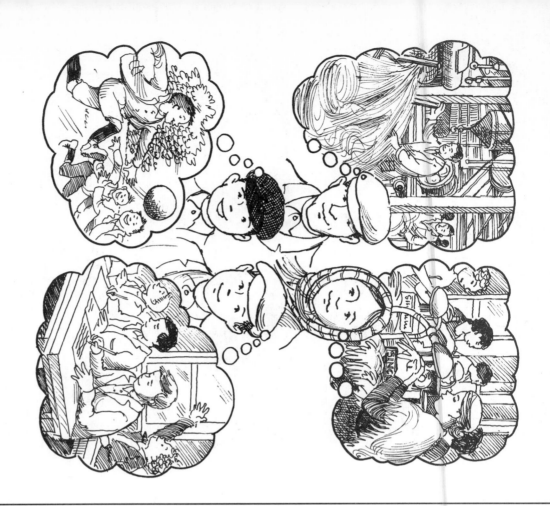

We're off to America.
We're on our way.
We want better lives and
good jobs for good pay.

Sea sprays in our faces,
and wind rocks the ship.
The uneasy ride makes us
sick the whole trip.

# The Man, the Boy, and the Donkey

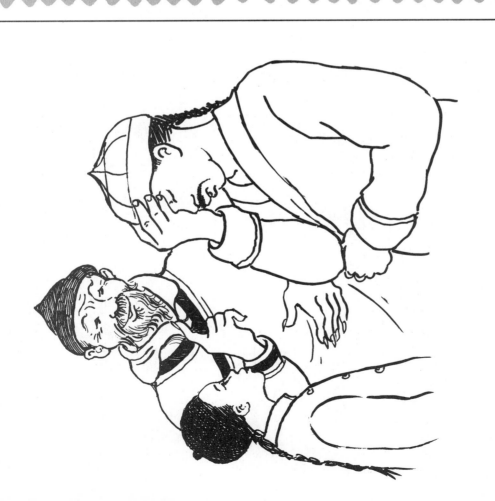

An old man had been following them. Now he came up to them and said, "Learn from this. Try to please everyone and you will please no one at all."

One day, a man and his son led a donkey to market. A farmer walked by and said, "Fools! Donkeys are to ride on!" On hearing this, the man put his son on the donkey's back.

The man and his son carried the donkey into the busy market. Just then, the donkey kicked its feet free and fell to the ground. Then it got up and ran off. The man and his son felt sad for their loss.

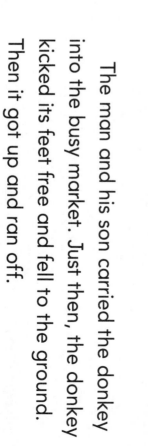

The man walked while his son rode.

They passed a group of men.

"Such a lazy boy!" said the men. "He makes his father walk while he rides!"

So the man and the son switched places.

The two picked up the donkey and carried it between them. All the way to town, people laughed and made fun of them.

Village women walked by. "How selfish!" they cried. "That man makes his poor son walk while he rests."

So the man pulled his son up onto the donkey beside him. They both rode.

Farther down the road, people cried out, "Shame on you for making that little donkey carry such a heavy load!"

The man and his son did not know what to do. So they got off the donkey.

# The Day the Sun Didn't Shine

"All right! I believe you!" said the hedgehog. He looked up to the sky and yelled, "I wish for the sun to come out! I will never again complain of its light!"

Instantly, heat and light filled the earth.

"Nicely done," remarked the toad.

And the sun never hid its light again.

7

"It's too bright out here," complained a hedgehog one day. "I'm getting a headache from all this sun. I wish the sun would take a break!"

"Be careful what you wish for," warned a toad who passed by.

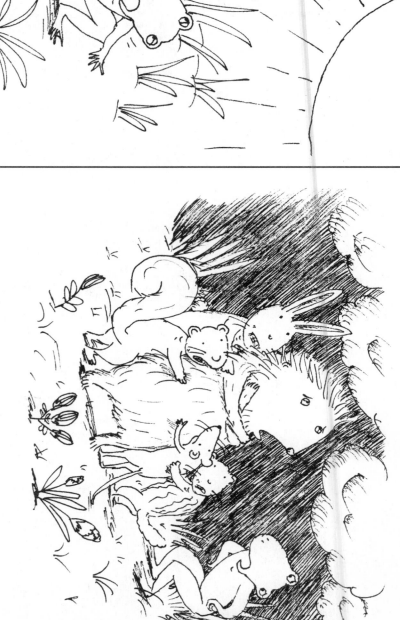

Animals huddled together for warmth. Flowers kept their petals tightly shut. Plants did not grow. Everyone felt tired and cross.

"I'm so tired that it's giving me a headache," complained the hedgehog.

"Is that so?" glared the toad.

That night, the sun set as usual. The sky grew dark, and just the tiniest sliver of moonlight shone. Then a big cloud covered even that. The night was as dark as the very deepest black.

"Impossible!" snapped the hedgehog. "The sun has nothing to do with all that."

"Just wait," said the toad. "You'll see."

Days went by, and the sun did not shine. The earth stayed covered in darkness.

The next day, the sun did not come out.
The sky stayed black, and the earth
was covered in darkness.

"Look what you've done!" cried the toad.
"Your wish has come true! Do you know
what this means?"

"It means no more headaches!"
sang the hedgehog, and he did
a little dance.

The toad snorted. "IT MEANS, NO
MORE HEAT," he shouted. "No more light.
No seeds growing and flowers in bloom."

# What's the Matter?

"Nice work!" said Professor Betty.

"You've learned that some kinds of matter can change with temperature. Now you know the three states of matter: *solid, liquid,* and *vapor* or *gas.* You win the bonus challenge!"

Professor Betty was eating a tuna fish sandwich when she heard people calling.

"Professor Betty! Professor Betty!"

Professor Betty looked up to find three of her students standing before her.

"How about when water's really hot?" asked the professor. "What's the matter then?"

"When water gets hot, it boils and turns into steam," said Tori. "Then matter is a vapor or gas."

"What's the matter?" asked the professor.
Michelle, Shiro, and Tori grinned.

"That's what you asked us in class this
morning," said Shiro. "Now we know!"

"Water that is very cold turns to ice,"
said Michelle. "That matter is a solid."

"When it's warm?" asked Professor Betty.

"Ice melts into water when it warms up,"
said Shiro. "Then matter is a liquid."

"Ah!" said Professor Betty.
"You solved my bonus questions!
What is the matter when it's cold?
What is the matter when it's warm?
What is the matter when it's hot?"

"We didn't understand at first," said Michelle. "Then at lunch, I bought an ice pop. I left it on the table, and it melted into a watery mess! Right then, I knew!"

"So, tell me," said the professor, "what's the matter when it's cold?"

# Pass the Chips!

George opened his own restaurant and put potato chips on the menu. In time, potato chips were packaged and sold in the New England states. Today, they are sold across the United States and all over the world!

It was a summer night in 1853.
At a restaurant in New York state,
chef George Crum was hard at work.
"Ah," said the chef. "Someone wants
a plate of my tasty French fries."

1

Word spread, and people came from
all over to taste George's new crispy fries.
He named them Saratoga Chips, because
the restaurant was in Saratoga Springs,
New York.

6

George made his best batch yet.

The fries were thick and golden brown.

But the customer was not happy.

"Take these back," complained the customer.

"They are too thick to eat."

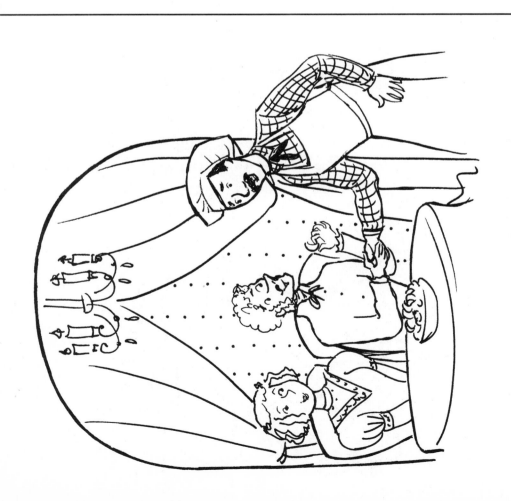

George thought the customer would be angry. To his surprise, the customer loved them! The customer ate the whole plateful and asked for more. Other diners began to ask for them, too.

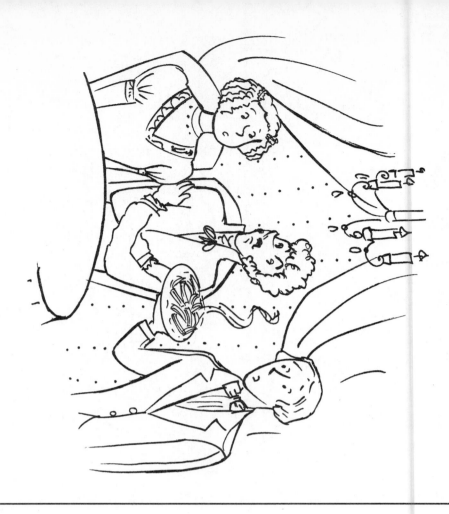

George made another batch right away. He cut the potatoes much thinner than before. Then he fried them. Again, the customer sent the fries back.

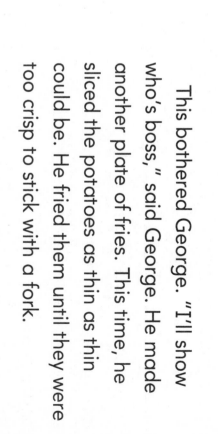

This bothered George. "I'll show who's boss," said George. He made another plate of fries. This time, he sliced the potatoes as thin as thin could be. He fried them until they were too crisp to stick with a fork.

# Tornado!

The News Gazette

TERRIBLE STORM HITS!

Scientists say this was one of the most dangerous tornadoes ever. It's hard to believe that one storm could cause so much harm.

It is late afternoon on May 3, 1999.
The air feels warm and sticky here in
Oklahoma. The sky grows very dark.
It is too dark for the middle of the day.

The tornado has passed now. We step
outside. All around us, the ground is
littered with bricks, wood, tables, and
beds. Cars and tractors lie upside down.
Trees are stripped of bark. Some trees
have snapped in half.

I look up and can't believe my eyes.
I see a thick, black cloud so huge it fills
the whole sky. From it comes a mighty,
spinning tunnel of wind. It is a tornado!

Many people hear the news that a
tornado is coming. As my family and I do,
they run to hide in cellars under the ground.
Staying underground until the storm ends
will save our lives.

The tornado stretches from the sky to the ground. It is thickest at the top, up in the clouds. It spins, a fierce tunnel of wind. It scatters everything in its path.

The tornado destroys as it races along. Roaring, it rips roofs off houses. The tornado blows apart homes made of brick and barns made of wood. The powerful wind throws trailers and trucks through the air.

# Man on the Moon

Neil and Buzz walked on the moon for almost three hours. Then they climbed back into the *Eagle*. The next day, they returned to the *Columbia* and headed home. On Earth, they had become heroes. In space, they had made an American dream come true.

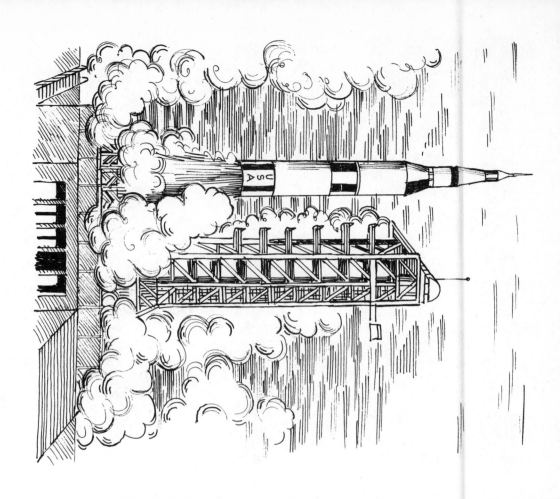

On July 16, 1969, three astronauts flew into space. They set out to do what no one had done before. They went to put a man on the moon.

Then Buzz Aldrin stepped out of the *Eagle*. Together, the two collected rocks and soil from the moon. They would bring these samples back to Earth for scientists to study.

On July 20, 1969, they did just that. Their spaceship had two parts. One part, the *Columbia*, took the astronauts into space. The other part, the *Eagle*, was made to land on the moon.

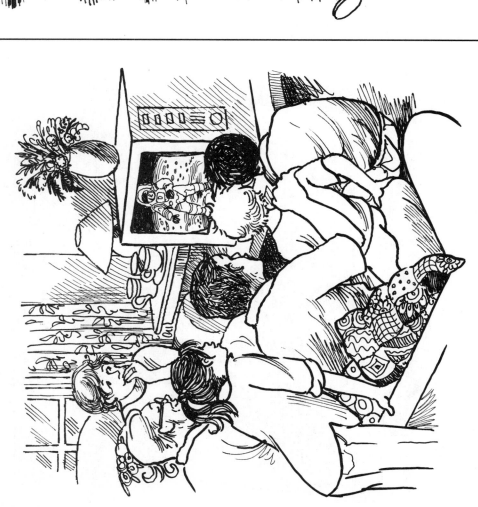

"That's one small step for man, one giant leap for mankind," he said. People all over the world heard Neil and saw that first step on the moon. A TV camera on the *Eagle* had recorded it.

One astronaut, Michael Collins, stayed on the *Columbia*. The other two, Neil Armstrong and Buzz Aldrin, climbed into the *Eagle*. They could see the moon. They steered the *Eagle* toward it.

Then came the words the world had been waiting to hear. "The *Eagle* has landed," said Neil Armstrong. Neil opened the door of the *Eagle*. He climbed down its ladder and stepped on the moon.

# Born to Fly

In June 1937, Amelia began a flight around the world. Before she could finish, Amelia's plane went down. Nine ships and 66 planes searched. None could find her. Today we remember Amelia's courage and skill.

The first time Amelia Earhart rode in a plane, she loved it. "By the time I got 200 to 300 feet off the ground," said Amelia, "I knew I had to fly."

For five years, Amelia continued to set records. Twice she flew from Hawaii to Washington, D.C. Ten pilots had died trying to make that flight

That first plane ride took place
in December 1920. Six days later,
Amelia took her first flying lesson.
Then she bought her first airplane.
She named her yellow plane *Canary*.

That June, Amelia crossed the Atlantic
Ocean in a small plane. She flew as a
passenger. Four years later, she flew across
by herself. Amelia became the first woman
to cross the Atlantic alone.

Almost at once, Amelia broke world records in flight. She became the first woman pilot to get a license. She flew higher and faster than anyone ever had.

Then, in 1928, Amelia received a phone call. It was from Captain H. H. Railey. "Amelia," he asked. "How would you like to be the first woman to fly across the Atlantic?" Amelia said, "Yes."

# A View From the Top

Meg collects some of the insects and plant life. Her work helps scientists around the world learn more about rainforest life.

When Meg Lowman was little, she loved to climb trees. She searched the branches for insects and flowers. Today Meg still spends lots of time in the treetops. It is her job.

Meg faces danger in the treetops, too. There are snakes, bats, and ants that sting. There are poison dart frogs and thorny vines to climb around.

Meg is a rainforest scientist. She studies rainforests all over the world. She finds out what kinds of insects live there. She learns how they affect plant life.

Way up high, Meg studies life that she can't see on the ground. She sees many plants, insects, and other living things. Nowhere else in the world are there so many.

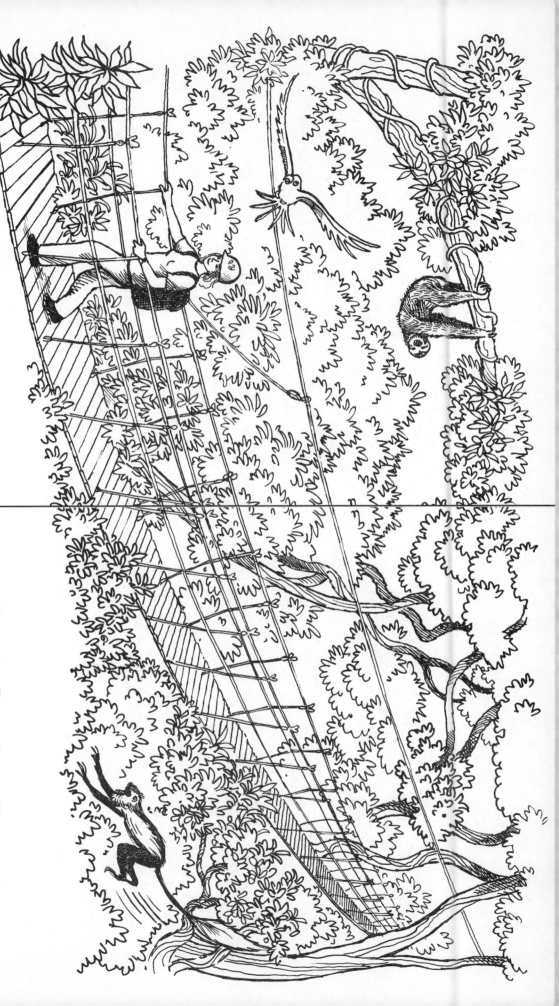

Meg doesn't just study life from
the ground. She climbs up high
in the trees. She and her helpers
have built a walkway up there.

Meg's walkway looks like a bridge.
It hangs from the trees on steel wires.
Meg wears a harness to keep her safe.
The harness has ropes and wires.
It keeps Meg from falling if she slips.

# Sal Fink

Mike Fink didn't have to go teach those pirates a lesson. They never got free from the ropes Sal had tied. And Sal and Mike Fink? They kept on riding the river.

⑦

Once there lived a man named Mike Fink. He ran a riverboat up and down the Mississippi and Ohio rivers. Folks say he was the roughest, toughest man ever to ride the water.

1

Sal waited until the pirates fell asleep. Then she burst free from the ropes. She tied up those pirates faster than a chipmunk runs from a coyote. Then Sal left the pirates behind and went home.

6

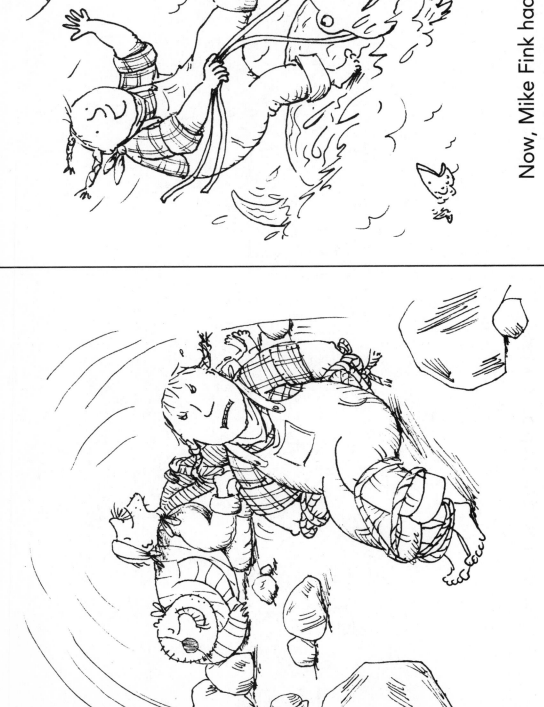

Now, Mike Fink had a daughter
named Sal. Sal Fink was as tough
as her daddy. She rode alligators
and never fell off. She rowed upstream
alone as fast as ten men could together.

Sal was hopping mad.
Those pirates had no idea
what a woman they'd caught.
They would soon find out.

Sal was special off the river, too.
She hunted, fished, and wrestled bears.
She kept two cubs with her for fun.

3

One day, Sal was hunting bobcats.
All of a sudden, pirates grabbed her!
They tied Sal up and took her to their
cave. They wanted Mike Fink to give
them a pile of money. Then they'd give
Sal back.

4